MW00887702

AUTHENTIC JAPANESE STEEL

Made in the USA
Monee, IL
11 August 2021

75431396R10072